SAUCES & SALSAS

SILVANA FRANCO

Tastes, traditions and over 75 international recipes,
with notes on their origins and uses

APPLE

A QUARTO BOOK

PUBLISHED BY THE APPLE PRESS
THE OLD BREWERY, 6 BLUNDELL STREET
LONDON N7 9BH

ISBN 1-85076-635-5

THIS BOOK WAS DESIGNED AND PRODUCED BY
QUARTO PUBLISHING PLC
THE OLD BREWERY
6 BLUNDELL STREET
LONDON N7 9BH

ART DIRECTOR: MOIRA CLINCH
DESIGN: DESIGN REVOLUTION
SENIOR ART EDITOR: LIZ BROWN
COPY EDITOR: BEVERLEY LEBLANC
HOME ECONOMIST: CAROL TENNENT
PICTURE RESEARCHER: SUSANNAH JAYES
PICTURE MANAGER: GIULIA HETHERINGTON
SENIOR EDITOR: SIAN PARKHOUSE
EDITORIAL DIRECTOR: MARK DARTFORD
PHOTOGRAPHER: PHILIP WILKINS
ILLUSTRATORS: AMANDA GREEN & ANDREW MORRIS

TYPESET IN GREAT BRITAIN BY CENTRAL SOUTHERN TYPESETTERS, EASTBOURNE
Printed in Singapore by Star Standard Industries Pte. Ltd.

CONTENTS

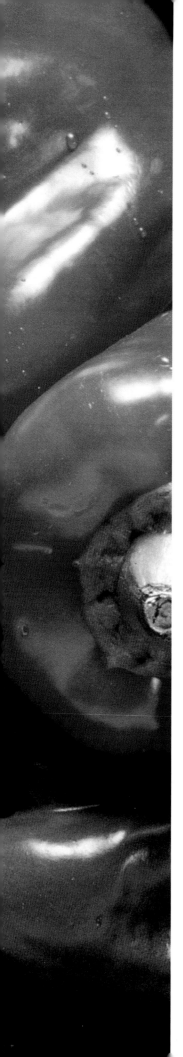

Salsas *and* Ketchups *from* Around *the* World

BROKEN INTO SEVEN CHAPTERS, EACH FOCUSING
ON THE CUISINE OF A DIFFERENT AREA OF THE
WORLD, THIS ECLECTIC COLLECTION OF RECIPES
CAPTURES THE ESSENCE OF INDIVIDUAL REGIONS,
WHILST ACKNOWLEDGING THE WORLD-WIDE FUSION
OF COOKERY INGREDIENTS AND STYLES.

Each chapter contains a selection of recipes
for ketchups, sauces and salsas, some of which
are based on traditional recipes, whilst others
are modern interpretations of the region's
style and flavours. All the recipes are simple
to use and if, in the case of some ketchups,
cooking time is fairly lengthy, the preparation
is minimal – and the results well worth taking
time over. As for the salsas, cooking times (if
any) are, in most cases, well under 30 minutes.

Ketchups and salsas are extremely flexible in
both their ingredients and uses, so once a
recipe has been mastered, experiment with
the spices and ingredients to mix and match
flavours to suit your tastes. Remember, there
are no rules!

From garlic and thyme to coriander and nutmeg, the flavours of the world add variety and spice to life.

Salsa

Colourful and flavoursome, hot and spicy or cool and refreshing, a salsa is a thing to savour – but what is it? Originating in Mexico, *salsa* simply means "sauce", and in Mexican terms that means fiery and tomatoey with plenty of fresh chillies, onion, coriander, garlic and salt. In other parts of the world, however, a salsa is more of a side dish – in Spain, for example, it is served as tapas alongside a handful of other small snacks.

Wherever it is created, a salsa is always a blend of chopped, diced or grated fruit and vegetables, and herbs characteristic of the region. Sometimes cooked, but most often raw, salsas can be dry, moist or saucy, but whatever the consistency, they are always served as one element of a meal, either to spice up or cool down the palate.

SERVING SALSAS

WITHOUT DOUBT, THE MOST POPULAR WAY TO SERVE
A SALSA IS AS A DIP. WHETHER AS A STARTER, PART OF A MEAL OR AS A SNACK, ALMOST ALL
SALSAS CAN BE PUT TO GOOD USE SERVED WITH A SELECTION OF TASTY MORSELS TO DIP WITH.
HERE ARE A FEW SUGGESTIONS OF WHAT TO SERVE WITH YOUR SALSA.

TORTILLA CHIPS

Available in a wide selection of flavours, from cheese corn chips to fiery nachos, tortilla chips are the best accompaniment to any tomato-based salsa such as Salsa Cruda and Instant Tomato Salsa .

CRUDITES

A selection of crunchy raw vegetables such as cauliflower florets, carrot batons and sticks of celery make delicious scoops for both creamy and spicy salsas. Prepare the vegetables as near to serving time as possible so they keep their bite.

ROASTED VEGETABLES

Delicious and easy to prepare, roasted vegetables are super for serving with hot or spicy salsas. Simply cut the vegetables into wedges, toss with a little oil and salt and roast at 200°C/400°F/Gas 6 for 45 minutes to 1 hour. Good choices include fresh plum tomatoes, aubergine, plus all root vegetables, especially parsnips and carrots.

POTATO SKINS

Crispy potato skins are delicious served with creamy salsas, and chilli- or onion-based salsas. Try substituting them for the tortilla chips served with the classic South American Salsa Con Queso . To make your own potato skins, bake 2 large (at least 250g/½lb potatoes) for 1 hour until soft. Halve the potatoes and scoop out the flesh to leave a shell about 1cm/½in thick. Cut each half into 6 wedges then deep fry in hot vegetable oil for 3–5 minutes until crisp and golden. Drain on kitchen paper and sprinkle lightly with salt or paprika. Serve hot.

CHEESE STRAWS

Buy cheese straws ready made or for a quick way to make your own, use a 250g/½lb packet of ready-made puff pastry. Lightly flour a work surface and sprinkle generously with freshly grated Parmesan cheese. Roll the pastry out on-to the surface until it is about 5mm/¼in thick. Cut into 1cm/½in wide strips about 14cm/6in long. Leave the strips flat or twist them a few times for a rope effect. Brush with a little milk and bake for 15 minutes at 200°C/400°F/ Gas 6 until crisp and golden. Allow to cool and serve warm or store in an air tight container for 2 or 3 days.

VEGETABLE CRISPS

You can, of course, buy potato crisps in a fan-tastic variety of flavours, but it is very simple to make your own and they taste much nicer. Simply peel a large potato and then shave off thin slices with the peeler. Deep fry in hot oil for 3–4 minutes until they rise to the surface. Scoop out with a slotted spoon and drain on kitchen paper before seasoning with salt and for extra kick, a little ground chilli. You can also get some surprisingly good results if you try this method with other root vegetables: carrots, parsnip, sweet potato, celeriac and beetroot are all delicious when sliced wafer thin and deep fried. Whatever vegetable you choose to use, it is better to fry them in batches as they have a tendency to stick together. This applies parti-cularly to starchy vegetables such as potatoes which may benefit from being soaked in cold water and then dried thoroughly before frying.

In the shady olive groves in Andalusia, the succulent fruits gently open.

9

STORING KETCHUPS

COOKED KETCHUPS WITH A HIGH VINEGAR CONTENT, SUCH AS THE
ENGLISH VARIETIES, CAN BE KEPT FOR AT LEAST SIX MONTHS, IF THE BOTTLES ARE CORRECTLY STERILIZED
AND SEALED TO PREVENT FERMENTATION OR THE DEVELOPMENT OF ANY TOXINS. SAFEGUARD KETCHUPS
THAT ARE INTENDED FOR LONG-TERM STORAGE AS FOLLOWS:

1 Preheat the oven to 110°C/225°F/Gas ¼. Wash the bottles and jars in warm soapy water and rinse well in clean water.

2 Place a wire rack in the bottom of a large saucepan and place the bottles and jars on it, making sure they are not touching each other or the sides of the pan.

Careful storage will ensure that the rich flavours of herbs and spices are not lost.

3 Pour in enough clean boiling water to cover the bottles, then bring it to the boil and boil rapidly for 10 minutes.

4 Carefully remove the bottles or jars and leave them upside down to drain on a clean towel.

5 Transfer the bottles or jars to the oven to dry out completely. Leave them in the oven until you are ready to fill them with ketchup. Take care not to have the oven temperature any higher than 110°C/225°F/Gas ¼ or there is a danger that the glass will crack.

6 Ladle the hot ketchup into the warm, dry jars, filling them to within 1cm/½in of the rim. Wipe the rims with a clean damp cloth, then seal the jars or bottles immediately.

7 Store the ketchups out of direct sunlight in a cool, dry place. Refrigerate once opened.

A pleasing array of jars filled with good things to eat.

HEAT SEALING

It is not essential to heat seal the ketchups if the jars have been properly sterilized and filled, however, this is another safety measure you can do to protect your ketchups. This method heats the contents to a very high temperature, killing off enzymes, which prevents fermentation and also forms a hermetic seal. To ensure a safe seal, use tongs to lower the bottles or jars into a large pan of boiling water with a wire rack in the bottom. Boil for 30 minutes, keeping the jar submerged by topping up the pan with boiling water. Carefully remove the jars and leave to cool for 12 hours. To check the seal, if the jar has a screwtop lid, it will be slightly concave; if you are using a glass-lidded clip-jar, gently try and lift the lid – if the seal is safe it will resist.

air-tight container.

KETCHUP

Always smooth and often spicy, a ketchup is a table condiment that brings a burst of flavour to everyday meals. It is incredibly versatile and can be used to enhance the flavour of any dish – a Jamaican ketchup, for example, tastes superb on a British banger. There are a number of ways to make ketchup, from the traditional style which contains a high percentage of vinegar and is packed into sterilized jars to be kept for a number of months, to the fresh saucy cross-breeds such as Israeli Sabra which need to be kept covered in the refrigerator for only two or three days.

A fine source of flavour, ketchups have been popular for over 300 years.

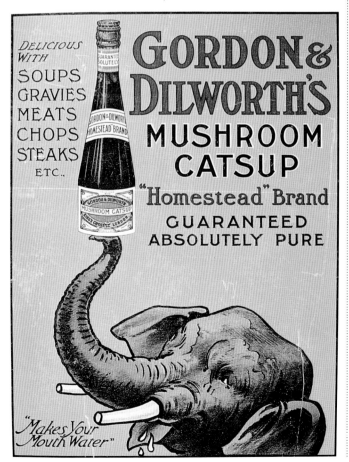

Ketchups have, in fact, been around since the 17th century under the names of *koechiap, catchup* and *catsup*, with the term *ketchup* finally entering the English dictionary about 1710. The most famous ketchup is, of course, the commercially made tomato variety, whose plastic squeezy bottle full of bright red sauce, can be found gracing the kitchen table of homes all over the world. Humble as it is, tomato ketchup brings life to tired food. After all, who would even consider eating a burger and fries without a good old dollop of ketchup on the side? So, imagine what a stir you can cause if you have a go at making your own.

What's in a name?

SALSA IS A GENERAL TERM FOR A
SAUCE, BUT THE FOLLOWING ARE MORE SPECIFIC VARIETIES.

ACAR OR AJTAR

Fruit or vegetable preserved in, or flavoured with, vinegar, spices and chilli.

BLATJANG

Thick and chunky blatjangs can be found in Southern Africa and Malaysia and are traditionally flavoured with prawns or shrimp paste.

CATSUP

The original ketchup, this term is still used in some regions.

CHOWCHOW

A sour salsa, that generally contains vinegar and spices, and vegetables rather than fruit.

KETCHUP

Thick and smooth fruit or vegetable sauce. Generally contains vinegar to help preserve it.

RELISH

Fairly impossible to define, every entry here may be classed as a relish.

SALSA

This translates into sauce, but any small dish made principally from fruit or vegetables, whether raw or cooked, may call itself a salsa.

SAMBAL

Usually a smooth paste. Often quite oily and spicy, always hot.

CHUTNEY

A thick ketchup that contains chunks of fruit or vegetables and often whole spices. Thought to have originated in India, chutney is a popular accompaniment to spicy curries.

PREPARATION TECHNIQUES

Take the plunge –
a top tip for
onion preparation.

SKINNING TOMATOES

There are two basic methods for peeling tomatoes. I am in favour of the first technique, mainly because of speed, but there is a noticeable difference in the texture and flavour of the tomato depending upon which method is used. Many, however, opt for the second method as it is easier to control.

1) Flame – Impale the tomato on a fork or skewer and hold in a naked flame over a gas ring or under a hot grill for a few seconds, turning the tomato until the skin blisters. Slip off the skins, and the flesh will still be firm. This method also works well for chillies.

2) Hot Water – Cut a small cross in the top of the tomatoes and place in a bowl. Pour over boiling water and leave for exactly 1 minute. Cool under running water, then slip off the skins.

DESEEDING TOMATOES

Remove the green stalk core and cut the tomatoes in half vertically. Use a teaspoon to scoop out the seeds.

PEELING ONIONS

Plunge whole onions into boiling water for exactly 1 minute. Cool under running water and the skins will have softened sufficiently to make peeling a lot easier.

PEELING GARLIC

If you have more than 2 or 3 garlic cloves to prepare, separate the cloves and remove the outer papery skins. Place the cloves in a small bowl and cover with warm water. Leave for a minute or 2, before draining. The skin will have softened, and peeling the cloves will be simpler.

Pungent garlic adds flavour to both ketchups and salsas, but preparation can be timely.

Roasting peppers truly brings out their natural sweetness.

ROASTING PEPPERS

Roasted Peppers are more often cooked under the grill than actually roasted in an oven. Although it is quicker to halve or quarter the peppers before roasting them, it is much better to keep them whole so that the delicious juices which are released during cooking are collected inside the pepper.

Arrange the whole peppers on a baking sheet or grill pan and place under a hot grill for 8–12 minutes, turning until the skin is blistered and blackened. Cover with a clean tea towel or place in a plastic bag for around 5 minutes so that the steam helps lift up the skin. Now pierce a hole in the bottom of the pepper and squeeze out the juice. Save the juice to add to a dressing or marinade for the peppers. Peel away the skin and halve the peppers. Remove the central stalk and seeds.

DESEEDING CHILLIES

Use a small sharp knife to halve the chillies lengthways then, with the tip of the knife, scrape away the seeds and white membrane. If you are sensitive to the pungent fumes of some chillies, you may find it easier to scrape the seeds out under cold running water.

CHOPPING CHIVES

Don't bother to chop chives in the way that you do other herbs. Instead, gather up a small bunch and quickly snip them with a pair of sharp kitchen scissors.

TOASTING SEEDS AND NUTS

Most nuts, seeds and some spices, in particular cumin, benefit from toasting as the dry heat really brings out the flavour. My preferred method is to stir-fry the ingredient in a large non-stick frying pan, without any oil, for between 2 and 5 minutes until it turns golden and releases its aroma.

Chopped or flaked nuts may also be placed under a hot grill or in a hot oven for a few minutes until golden, the latter giving the most even colouring of all methods.

STONING AVOCADOS

Cut the avocado in half lengthways, cutting right through to the stone. Hold the avocado in both hands and twist in opposite directions, whilst pulling the two halves apart. Hold the half

Fiery chillies need careful handling, even when they are dried.

containing the stone in one hand and pierce the stone firmly with a sharp knife. Lift up the knife and the stone will come away with it.

CUTTING CORN KERNELS

Remove the kernels from the corn cob either before or after cooking, depending upon your use – leave the kernels on the cob for barbecuing but cut them off before boiling.

Strip off the green husky leaves and silky threads. Slice off the stalk at the base. Hold the cob upright on a board, and cut down using a large sharp knife. The kernels will slice off easily.

GRINDING SEEDS AND PASTES

The traditional way to grind hard seeds, or pound moist ingredients into a paste, is by using a pestle and mortar. They can be made from a number of materials, but are often porcelain or marble. The end of the pestle and the base of the mortar are usually unglazed or slightly coarse to create friction between the two. Of course, those in a hurry can always use a mini food processor.

A pestle and mortar is indispensable when crushing small seed pods.

BREAD STICKS

Rich pickings: sun-ripened tomatoes offer the perfect salsa base.

Italian-style *grissini* bread sticks are a super crisp snack for serving with every kind of salsa. Readily available from grocers, they now come in a number of thicknesses and flavours such as sesame seed and cheese. But if you fancy having a go at making them yourself, here is a simple recipe.

MAKES 30

225g • 8oz strong white flour, plus extra for rolling	*1 tsp salt*
	4 fl oz warm water
7g • ¼oz easy-blend yeast	*2 tbsp olive oil*

❶ Preheat the oven to 230°C/450°F/Gas 8. Sieve the flour and salt into a bowl. Stir in the yeast and make a well in the centre.

❷ Add the water and olive oil and bring together to make a firm dough. Knead for 5 minutes until smooth.

❸ Rub a little oil into the surface of the dough. Cover with a clean tea towel and leave in a warm place to rise for 40 minutes.

❹ Knead the dough lightly then roll out onto a floured surface to make a rectangle about 14cm/6in wide and 5mm/¼in thick. Cut the rectangle widthways into 30 thin strips.

❺ Roll each strip into a long thin sausage about 25cm/10in long. Arrange on a baking sheet and cook in the oven for 15 minutes until crisp and golden. Allow to cool then store in an air-tight container.

EUROPE

OF ALL THE REGIONS *covered in this book, Europe, and in particular England, has the most extensive collection of traditional ketchups, some of which can be traced back hundreds of years to ancient recipes. On the whole, these sauces tend to be an uncomplicated blend of only two or three main ingredients simmered in a spiced vinegar solution, which, if stored correctly, will keep for a number of months.*

When it comes to salsas, however, the flavours of the Mediterranean come into their own with Greek Calamata olives, feta cheese, Italian plum tomatoes, fresh oregano, olive oils and French mustard and garlic, making warm, summer-tasting salsa combinations.

European Ingredients

A colourful array of freshly picked produce in a Venician open-air market.

BALSAMIC VINEGAR

Made only in one region of northern Italy, traditional balsamic vinegar is aged in oak casks for 10–20 years to produce a dark syrupy vinegar that is sweet enough to be served straight from the bottle as a salad dressing. Although fairly pricy, just a small splash enlivens tomato salsas, grilled fish and vegetables, and brings a new dimension to almost any vinegar-based English-style ketchup.

OLIVES

All olives as we know them have been cured, as they are very bitter if eaten straight from the tree. Green olives are picked and pickled before they are ripe, and are best served as a cocktail appetizer, and as such can be bought packed with delicious stuffings such as pimiento, garlic and almonds. Black olives are more suitable for cooking with, and often grace pizzas and pasta sauces, as well as salads and salsas. Greek, French and Italian olives are all equally popular but whichever type you buy, if you buy them loose rather than packed in brine or oil, keep them in the refrigerator and eat within three days.

OREGANO

Closely related to French marjoram, but rather more powerful, Italian oregano is, according to some, at its best when dried. Alongside basil, it is the herb most associated with Italian cookery and is an essential flavouring of the classic tomato sauce used for both pasta and pizzas.

MUSTARD

Most of the mustards available are now made from ground brown mustard seed, as opposed to the once-popular, and much hotter, black seeds. Often the seeds are only partly ground, resulting in the mild, coarse-grained varieties that are currently so fashionable. There are many specialized mustards around such as Dijon, and tarragon, which are most often served with meats but can also be stirred into simple vinaigrettes, mayonnaises and soft cheese for delicious dressings.

TOMATOES

With so many varieties of tomatoes available it is difficult to know which to choose. Unfortunately, many are grown for appearance, rather than flavour, and are often watery and bland. If you

A French stall displays its wonderfully fragrant spices.

can, opt for ripe, Italian plum tomatoes or the much smaller sweet cherry tomatoes. Avoid the large hot-house type that look so perfect and appetizing, as the flavour, or lack of it, will probably be disappointing. Keep an eye open for yellow tomatoes, which not only look lovely but taste delicious, too.

DRIED TOMATO SALSA

TO DRY TOMATOES

This is the most time-consuming salsa in the book, as first you must dry the tomatoes (see right). Dry them in large batches and store in plain, top-quality olive oil until you are ready to use them – don't, however, be tempted to flavour the oil with any herbs as it will detract from the pure flavour of the tomatoes. Drying them truly brings out the sweetness in all varieties of tomatoes, and they can then be used to enhance a whole host of dishes, such as salsas, salads, risottos – my absolute favourite is a freshly baked mozzarella-covered pizza topped with home-dried tomatoes and a handful of torn basil leaves.

Serve this sunny-tasting Italian salsa with a bowl of black olives, a slab of Gorgonzola cheese and some warm garlic bread for a rustic starter or alfresco lunch

SERVES 2

12 home-dried tomato halves, roughly chopped (see below)
2 purple shallots, finely chopped
2 garlic cloves, finely chopped
handful roughly torn basil leaves
3 tbsp olive oil
2 tbsp balsamic vinegar
salt

Toss all the ingredients together with salt to taste in a bowl and serve within about 2 hours. This is best eaten at room temperature.

The idea is to dry the tomatoes, not cook them, so keep an eye on them while they are in the oven, turning them occasionally and removing any that are ready before the others. They will shrivel up but should still be soft and not too papery. Because of the different sizes of tomatoes and performances of individual ovens, the process can take anything from 6 to 10 hours.

Dry as many tomatoes as you can fit into your oven at one time. In my oven, I find 20 tomatoes is about right. If you want to store the dried tomatoes in olive oil, layer them in sterilized jars, cover with the oil, seal and store for up to 6 months.

INGREDIENTS

tomatoes
coarse sea salt
extra-virgin olive oil, for bottling

❶ Preheat the oven to its lowest setting. Rinse the tomatoes well and cut them in half. Scoop out the seeds and discard.
❷ Place them cut-side down on kitchen paper for 10–15 minutes to remove the excess moisture.
❸ Lightly sprinkle the inside of the tomato halves with salt and arrange them closely, but not touching, on 2 wire racks, cut sides down. Transfer to the oven.
❹ If your oven allows it, keep the door slightly ajar by propping it open with a metal skewer.

Tomato Salsa

RHUBARB KETCHUP

Keep this stored in a cool dark place for at least a month before using to allow the flavours to mature.

MAKES 1.8 LITRES/3 PINTS

1kg • 2lb fresh rhubarb
175ml • 6fl oz freshly squeezed orange juice
2 large onions, roughly chopped
1l • 1¾pt malt vinegar
800g • 26oz light brown sugar

1 tsp salt
1 tsp allspice berries
1 tsp black/brown mustard seeds
1 tsp black peppercorns

❶ Rinse the rhubarb stalks well, then cut them into 2.5cm/ 1in lengths. Place in a large saucepan with the orange juice, onions, vinegar, sugar, salt and spices.
❷ Heat gently, stirring until the sugar dissolves. Cover and simmer on the lowest heat for 1½ hours until the mixture is pulpy, stirring occasionally.
❸ Strain the mixture through a fine non-metallic sieve, then pour immediately into hot sterilized bottles. Seal and store.

ENGLISH ORCHARD APPLE KETCHUP

Use a small, flavoursome variety of apple for this ketchup: Cox's Orange Pippins, Braeburns and Royal Galas are very good choices, but you can make use of whatever type you have available.

MAKES 1.2 LITRES/2 PINTS

2kg • 4lb apples, cored and roughly chopped
1 large onion, roughly chopped
600ml • 1½pt white vinegar
1 tbsp salt
1 tsp whole cloves
1 cinnamon stick
200g • 7oz sugar

❶ Place the apples, onion, salt, cloves, cinnamon and vinegar in a large pan. Bring to the boil then cover and simmer for 1½ hours, stirring occasionally, until pulpy.
❷ Strain through a fine non-metallic sieve, then return to the pan and put over a low heat. Stir in the sugar until dissolved. Bring to the boil and boil rapidly for 5 minutes, then immediately pour into hot sterilized bottles. Seal and store.

SPANISH ONION SALSA

If you don't have the large, mild-tasting Spanish onions to hand, use 2 regular onions in place of each Spanish one.

SERVES 6

25g • 1oz butter
2 tbsp olive oil
4 Spanish onions, thickly sliced
2 tbsp capers
4 anchovies in oil, roughly chopped
2 tbsp red wine vinegar
2 tbsp chopped fresh parsley seasoning

❶ Heat the butter and oil in a large pan and add the onions. Cook very gently for 20–30 minutes until softened and golden brown.
❷ Transfer to a serving dish and stir in the capers, anchovies, vinegar and parsley.
❸ Season to taste and serve warm or at room temperature. Do not refrigerate.

FRENCH MUSTARD SALSA

Make this salsa up to a day in advance and store in the fridge until ready to serve.

SERVES 4

250g • 8oz fine French beans, trimmed
115g • 4oz blanched whole almonds

2 tbsp walnut oil
1 tbsp white wine vinegar
1 tbsp wholegrain mustard
salt

❶ Cut the beans into 2.5cm/1in lengths and plunge into a pan of boiling salted water for 3–5 minutes until just tender. Drain in a colander, then cool under cold running water. Drain well on kitchen paper.
❷ Place the almonds in a heated wok or frying pan and stir-fry for a few minutes until golden. Place in bowl with the beans.
❸ Whisk together the oil, vinegar, mustard and a little salt, then toss together with the beans and nuts. Transfer to a bowl and leave to cool, then cover and chill until required.

ROASTED GARLIC SALSA

Don't be put off by the quantity of garlic involved in this salsa – the slow roasting mellows the pungency of the cloves, producing a melt-in-the-mouth sweetness. Serve this salsa with toasted country-style bread and a simple tomato salad for a sophisticated starter.

SERVES 4

4 garlic bulbs
2 rosemary sprigs
6 tbsp olive oil
2 tbsp chopped fresh sage

2 tbsp chopped fresh flat-leaf parsley
coarse sea salt

❶ Preheat the oven to 170°C/325°F/Gas 3. Place the garlic bulbs and rosemary sprigs in a roasting tin and drizzle with 4 tbsp of the oil and 4 tbsp of water.
❷ Sprinkle with a little sea salt and roast for 45 minutes, until the cloves are very soft. Cover the pan with foil if the bulbs start to become too brown.
❸ Leave the bulbs to cool for a few minutes then carefully squeeze the whole cloves out of their papery skins. Put in a bowl and toss with the chopped herbs and remaining olive oil. Serve warm or at room temperature.

French Mustard Salsa

ITALIAN KETCHUP

This mouth-watering ketchup tastes particularly good with char-grilled fish.

MAKES 1.2 LITRES/2 PINTS

1 large aubergine, roughly chopped

6 large ripe tomatoes, roughly chopped

1 cooking apple, cored and roughly chopped

1 large onion, roughly chopped

2 garlic cloves, halved

475ml • 6fl oz red wine vinegar

200g • 7oz soft brown sugar

5 star anise

handful fresh basil leaves

1 tsp salt

❶ Place the aubergine, tomatoes, apple, onion, garlic, vinegar, sugar, star anise, basil and salt in a large saucepan.

❷ Bring to the boil, then lower the heat, cover and simmer for 1½ hours until thick and pulpy, stirring occasionally.

❸ Strain the mixture through a fine non-metallic sieve, then immediately pour into hot sterilized bottles. Seal and store.

MUSHROOM KETCHUP

This is a versatile condiment and ingredient and can be added to soups and gravies for extra flavour, or used in place of soy sauce in stir-fries and rice dishes. If decanted into sealed and sterilized bottles, this ketchup will keep for a number of months.

MAKES 600ML/1 PINT

*1kg • 2lb large fresh
   mushrooms
50g • 2oz salt
600ml • 1pt red wine vinegar
1 tbsp ground allspice*

*1cm • ½in piece root ginger,
   roughly chopped
2 mace blades
1 shallot, finely chopped*

❶ Layer the mushrooms and salt in a lidded Kilner jar. Close the lid and leave for 2 days, stirring twice each day.
❷ Empty the contents of the jar into a large saucepan with the remaining ingredients. Cover and simmer for 30 minutes, stirring occasionally. Strain the mixture through a fine non-metallic sieve, then immediately pour into hot sterilized bottles. Seal and store.

MEDITERRANEAN SALSA

Serve this Mediterranean salsa warm
or at room temperature as part of a meal, or toss it
into a pan of freshly cooked pasta for a super light
lunch or supper dish.

SERVES 4

1 large aubergine
4 long shallots
2 plum tomatoes
1 tbsp olive oil
salt and freshly ground
   black pepper

FOR THE DRESSING
3 tbsp olive oil
juice of ½ lemon
1 tbsp chopped fresh oregano

❶ Preheat the grill to high. Slice the aubergine into
1cm/½in rounds. Quarter the shallots and tomatoes, then
place on a foil-lined grill pan with the aubergine. Brush with
olive oil and sprinkle lightly with salt.
❷ Place the vegetables under the grill for 8–10 minutes,
turning once, until tender and lightly charred. Cut the
aubergine slices into cubes and place in a large bowl with
the shallots and tomatoes.
❸ Quickly whisk together the dressing ingredients and
pour over the warm vegetables. Toss well together and
season to taste.

BRAMBLE KETCHUP

This is a great way to make good use of leftover hedgerow fruit such as blackberries and raspberries, and tastes superb served with a Cheddar cheese ploughman's lunch. Make sure the cheese you pair it with is well matured and robust, or the flavours of the ketchup will take over.

MAKES 1.2 LITRES/2 PINTS

2kg • 4lb blackberries
800g • 26oz white sugar
600ml • 1pt white wine vinegar
1 tsp ground cloves
1 tsp ground allspice
1 cinnamon stick

If you prefer a completely smooth ketchup, use whole spices and after cooking, strain the ketchup through a fine non-metallic sieve to remove the spices and pips.

❶ Place the blackberries, sugar, vinegar and spices in a pan. Bring to the boil, stirring until the sugar dissolves. Cover and simmer gently for 1 hour.

❷ Remove the cinnamon stick, then immediately pour the mixture into hot sterilized bottles. Seal and store.

BLACK OLIVE
AND PLUM TOMATO SALSA

For a delicious starter or light supper dish, place a 1cm/½in thick slice of rinded soft goat's cheese on a thick slice of country bread. Grill until it is bubbling and golden, then serve immediately with a big spoonful of this fragrant salsa on the side.

SERVES 4

6 plum tomatoes, roughly diced	1 tbsp balsamic vinegar
150g • ⅓lb Kalamata olives, left whole	1 garlic clove, finely chopped
6 spring onions, thinly sliced	1 tbsp chopped fresh basil
2 tbsp olive oil	salt and freshly ground black pepper

❶ Place the tomatoes and olives in a serving bowl and toss well together. Sprinkle over the spring onions.
❷ Whisk together the olive oil, balsamic vinegar, garlic, basil and plenty of seasoning. Drizzle over the salsa and serve immediately.

non fl.

Cogia

A

Kotore

Paganfu

Mar

Fachu

Trebizon
du.

Natolia

Co

Rey

Calla

Mofu

Ciprus

Persia

Saura

Siras

Mocha

dacb.

Medina

gyptus

Congas

Mecha

Geogun

Arabia.

Quifibi Calsiate

Zibit

Fartach

Aden

Bi

igide

Vella

Zauora

Chix
uno.

THE MIDDLE EAST

FROM A CULINARY POINT *of view, the Middle East not only covers the southern Asia region, stretching from Turkey down to Yemen, but also encapsulates the North African countries of Morocco, Algeria, Libya and Egypt. The food is hearty and well balanced with grains, beans and pulses forming the staples of the diet. Although flavoursome ingredients such as tahini paste, made from sesame seeds, dried fruit, olives, nuts, garlic and yogurt all feature strongly, hot food does not play a key role in the cooking of the region, and the use of the chilli is relatively minimal.*

Street food is very popular, with vendors selling local specialities, such as flat bread packed with onion salsa, or two or three falafel (fried chickpea patties) splashed with a spicy sauce.

MIDDLE EASTERN INGREDIENTS

Everyday life for the vendors in this Egyptian street bazaar.

CORIANDER

Both the seed and leaf of this herb are edible, and you will also see the leaf called cilantro. Found all over the Middle East, particularly in Morocco, the small seeds are round and hard, and, like cumin, are available both whole and ground. I recommend, however, that you buy only the whole seeds and pound them lightly in a mortar with a pestle just before using.

As a fresh leaf, coriander has an aromatic flavour that can be matched with almost anything. Pick the leaves from the stalk and toss them whole or roughly chopped into raw salsa, or stir into cooked sauces towards the end of the cooking time. It is used extensively in the Middle East in dishes such as couscous.

CUMIN SEEDS

A favourite flavouring in North Africa, cumin also appears extensively in Asian cooking. A small seed, it is sold both whole and ground, and like most spices should be roasted, toasted or fried rather than added raw to a dish. Cumin has a subtle flavour and can be used generously.

Olive oil

Not only a favourite of the Mediterranean, olive oil is extensively used in the Middle East as well. Extra-virgin olive oil is from the first pressing of the olives and as such is the purest and most flavoursome variety. It is also the most expensive – by quite a margin – of all types of olive oil, with many given names such as simply olive oil, light olive oil or pure olive oil. These oils have been refined more and have less character than the extra-virgin, but are fine for cooking with. Save your special top-quality extra-virgin olive oil for raw salsas and salad dressings, as a high temperature such as that required for frying destroys most of the flavour which you have paid extra for.

Tahini paste

This thick oily paste is simply crushed sesame seeds. Usually packed into a glass jar, it separates during storage and needs a stiff beating before use. An essential ingredient in many Middle Eastern dishes such as hummus and falafel, tahini paste is also delicious added to ketchups, soups and stocks.

Yoghurt

Yoghurt is an important ingredient in the Middle East. Often used as the base in marinades and soups, it adds a refreshing tang to otherwise bland dishes. Thick natural yoghurt is usually made from cows milk to which live bacteria cultures have been added, and is widely available from grocery stores.

Spices have always played a major role in Middle Eastern cuisine.

FATTOUSH

This popular Lebanese salsa has pieces of
crisply toasted Middle Eastern flat bread, such as pitta,
tossed in just before serving.

SERVES 4–6

1 cucumber, diced
1 large red pepper, cored,
   deseeded and diced
4 ripe tomatoes, diced
75g • 2½oz full-flavoured black
   olives, such as any oily Greek
   or Spanish variety
bunch spring onions, thickly
   sliced on the diagonal

2 tbsp chopped fresh flat-leaf
   parsley
2 pitta breads, toasted until
   crisp and golden
juice of ½ lemon
3 tbsp olive oil
salt and freshly ground black
   pepper

❶ Toss together the cucumber, pepper, tomatoes, olives,
onions and parsley in a large bowl.
❷ Break the pittas into bite-sized pieces and add to the salsa.
❸ Whisk together the lemon juice, olive oil and plenty of
seasoning. Pour over the salad, toss well together and serve
immediately.

SABRA

This Israeli dish is a cross between a ketchup
and a salsa. It is often served as a dip for biscuits and bread
with a *mezze*, a selection of small dishes served together
as a starter to a main meal.

SERVES 2

1 ripe avocado
1 green pepper, cored, deseeded
   and finely diced
1 small onion, finely diced
2 tbsp white wine vinegar

1 tbsp fresh lemon juice
180g • 6oz Greek-style yogurt
salt and freshly ground black
   pepper

❶ Halve, skin and stone the avocado, then mash it until it is
smooth in a large bowl.
❷ Add the pepper, onion, vinegar, lemon juice and yogurt to
the avocado and gently stir together, making sure the avocado
is well coated.
❸ Season to taste. Cover and chill until ready to serve.

Fattoush

HARISSA

This condiment is used in North Africa, particularly in Morocco, where a small amount is always served on the side with couscous. If you prefer, mix it with a smooth tomato sauce to make a less-powerful ketchup.

SERVES 10

10 fresh red chillies	*1 tsp coriander seeds*
1 red pepper	*1 tsp coarse sea salt*
4 garlic cloves, roughly chopped	*3 tbsp white wine vinegar*
1 tsp ground cumin	*2 tbsp olive oil*

❶ Deseed and roughly chop the chillies and pepper.
❷ Place the chillies and peppers in a mortar with the garlic, ground cumin and coriander seeds and grind to a paste with the pestle. You can use a food processor if you prefer.
❸ Stir in the salt, vinegar and olive oil, cover and keep in the fridge for up to a week. This freezes well.

TAHINI SAUCE

This sauce is used at Middle Eastern dining tables and as a flavouring in countless dishes. Mix it with thick plain yogurt to make a creamy dip for crudités or potato crisps.

SERVES 6

2 garlic cloves, roughly chopped
150g • ⅓lb tahini (sesame) paste
½ tsp ground coriander seeds
½ tsp ground cumin
juice of 1 lemon
salt and freshly ground black pepper

❶ Place the garlic, tahini paste, coriander and cumin in a blender or food processor. Whiz together for a minute, then, with the motor running, gradually add the lemon juice and 50ml/2fl oz water.

❷ Season well to taste. Transfer to a glass jar or plastic tub, seal and chill until ready to serve. This will keep in the fridge for up to 10 days.

FRIED GARLIC *AND* CHICKPEA SALSA

Serve this salsa with a selection of salads as part of a meal, or toss with a little Greek-style yogurt and eat with pitta bread for a delicious light lunch.

SERVES 4–6

2 tbsp vegetable oil
2 garlic cloves, thinly sliced
1 tsp cumin seeds
300g • 10oz canned chickpeas,
    drained and rinsed

2 tbsp chopped fresh mint
2 tbsp chopped fresh coriander
juice of 1 lime
salt and freshly ground black
    pepper

❶ Heat the oil in a small frying pan and gently cook the garlic and cumin seeds for 5 minutes, stirring occasionally, until the garlic is softened but not coloured.
❷ Place the chickpeas nd stir in the fried garlic mixture, chopped mint and coriander and the lime juice.
❸ Season to taste and serve while still warm, or cover and chill in the fridge until required.

ZHOUG

Also known as *zhoog* or *zhug*, this is a hot condiment from Yemen, where chillies are very popular. Spoon it into soups and dips or drizzle it over falafel (fried chickpea patties). It can be kept in the fridge for up to 10 days, but is most pungent the day it is made.

SERVES 10

6 garlic cloves, roughly chopped
6 green chillies, deseeded and
   roughly chopped
2 tomatoes, peeled, deseeded
   and roughly chopped
8 tbsp chopped fresh flat-leaf
   parsley

8 tbsp chopped fresh coriander
1 tbsp ground cumin
2 tbsp olive oil
2 tbsp lemon juice
salt and freshly ground black
   pepper

❶ Place the garlic and chillies in a blender or food processor and whiz together until well blended.
❷ Add the tomatoes, parsley, coriander and cumin and whiz again, then, with the motor running, slowly pour in the olive oil and lemon juice to make a smooth, thick sauce.
❸ Season well to taste. Transfer to a glass jar or plastic tub, seal and chill for at least an hour before serving.

AUBERGINE *AND* TAHINI
KETCHUP

Barbecues are very popular throughout the Middle East and this sauce is served as a fantastic accompaniment to grilled vegetables, chicken and meat. Stored in the fridge, covered, it will keep for 2 to 3 days.

SERVES 4

*1 large aubergine, halved
  lengthways*
2 tbsp olive oil
2 tbsp tahini (sesame) paste

2 garlic cloves, crushed
juice of ½ lemon
2 tbsp chopped fresh coriander
*salt and freshly ground black
  pepper*

❶ Preheat the grill or light the barbecue. Grill the aubergine halves for about 30 minutes, turning once until softened.

❷ Peel and discard the skin from the aubergine. Purée the flesh in a blender or food processor and transfer to a bowl. Stir in the olive oil, tahini paste, garlic, lemon juice and coriander. Season well to taste.

SPICY ORANGE SALSA

You'll find this zesty salsa served alongside
grilled fish and meat in Turkey. It tastes best served
at room temperature.

SERVES 4

3 large oranges, peeled and
  segmented
1 red onion, finely chopped
1 firm tomato, deseeded and cut
  into tiny dice

FOR THE DRESSING
2 tbsp olive oil
2 tbsp red wine vinegar
1 tsp chilli powder
2 tbsp chopped fresh thyme
salt and freshly ground black
  pepper

❶ Cut each orange segment into 3 even, bite-sized pieces,
then place them in a serving bowl with the onion and tomato
and gently toss together.
❷ Whisk together the dressing ingredients with a fork until
well blended. Season to taste and pour over the salad.
❸ Toss the salsa together well, cover and leave to rest for 1–4
hours, until ready to serve.

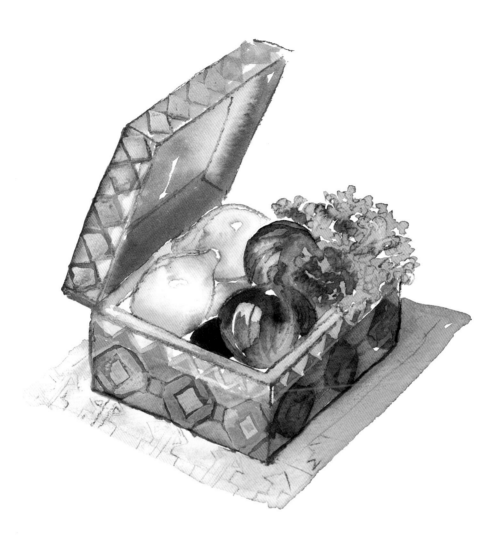

Feta *and* Olive Salsa

For a simple, tasty lunch, pile the
salsa on top of thick slices of toasted bread and drizzle
with the lemon-oil dressing.

SERVES 2

1 large ripe avocado, cubed
2 large ripe tomatoes, cubed
100g • 4oz black olives
1 red onion, roughly chopped
100g • 4oz feta cheese, cubed

1 tbsp chopped fresh parsley
2 tbsp olive oil
juice of a lemon
seasoning

❶ Place the avocado, tomatoes, olives, onion and feta in a
serving bowl and toss well together.
❷ Whisk together the parsley, olive oil, lemon juice and
seasoning and drizzle over the feta salsa. Serve immediately.

TABBOULEH

This classic Lebanese dish is made with bulgar wheat, also labelled as cracked wheat. It is generally on sale precooked and dried so it simply needs rehydrating with boiling water.

SERVES 4–6

125g • ¼lb bulgar wheat	*4 tbsp chopped fresh mint*
2 tomatoes, chopped	*juice of 1 lemon*
2 garlic cloves, finely chopped	*3 tbsp olive oil*
1 red onion, finely chopped	*salt and freshly ground black*
125g • ¼lb feta cheese, crumbled	*pepper*
* or diced*	

❶ Put the bulgar wheat in a large bowl and cover with boiling water. Set aside for 20 minutes until the grains have swollen and absorbed most of the water. Drain very well, squeeze out any excess moisture with your hands and return to the bowl.

❷ Stir in the tomatoes, garlic, onion, feta cheese, mint, lemon juice and olive oil. Mix well together, season to taste and serve. Cover and chill until ready to serve.

APRICOT DUKKAH

Dukkah is a nutty Egyptian dish that is sold by street vendors in little paper cones. I've added dried apricots and a few extra spices to turn it into a savoury salsa that can be kept in an air-tight container for a number of weeks. For added piquancy, stir in a little lemon juice, chopped red onion and garlic when you are ready to serve.

SERVES 4–6

125g • ¼lb hazelnuts, roughly chopped
4 tbsp sesame seeds
1 tsp coriander seeds
1 tsp cumin seeds
1 tbsp chopped fresh thyme
1 tbsp chopped fresh mint
150g • ⅓lb ready-to-eat dried apricots, roughly chopped
salt and freshly ground black pepper

❶ Place the nuts, sesame seeds, coriander seeds and cumin seeds in a large, heated frying pan or wok and stir-fry for 5–10 minutes until the nuts and seeds are golden.
❷ Transfer the nuts and seeds to a food processor with the thyme and mint and half of the apricots, and pulse together until finely chopped and crumbly.
❸ Transfer the mixture to a bowl. Stir in the remaining pieces of apricot and season to taste.

AFRICA

DIFFERENT COUNTRIES AND REGIONS *of Africa*

each have varied culinary characteristics. In certain areas, there are limited food resources –whether the country has suffered a natural disaster or has poor-quality land. In other areas, however, the food is hearty, wholesome, healthy and very tasty. Not unlike the rest of the world, Africa is absorbing the flavours of many other countries, such as those from South America, and producing a style of food that is now every bit as innovative as that found in the other major continents.

AFRICAN INGREDIENTS

An African market provides plenty of fresh, delicious produce.

OKRA

Also known as ladies fingers, bhindi, okro and ochroes, this green finger-shaped vegetable plays a key role in the cooking of many African, Caribbean and Asian countries. If not cooked thoroughly, however, it has a tendency towards stickiness which some find unpleasant. Before cooking, wash and dry it carefully, then trim off the ends. Okra is especially good stewed with other vegetables, as in the classic gumbo from the southern American states.

PALM OIL

Only available in specialist stores, palm oil is a bright red oil with a very distinct flavour. Use it in small quantities to enhance soups, salsas and sauces. If you do not have access to any, use ordinary sunflower or corn oil with a little turmeric added for flavour and colour.

PLANTAIN

Even though it is a member of the banana family, a plantain cannot be eaten raw. Instead it should be fried, boiled or baked. Plantains, however, can be used at any stage of ripeness from green through to black, and, like bananas, they become sweeter as they ripen. To make crisp plantain chips, the plantain must be hard and green, but for baking or boiling it should be ripe and yellow.

The bright, jewel-like colours of these African spices provide a stunning display.

FRESH SHRIMP SALSA

This simple salsa makes a wonderful snack. If you have difficulty sourcing palm oil, use vegetable oil and add 1 tsp ground turmeric.

SERVES 4

2 tbsp palm oil
1 small onion, finely chopped
2 fresh red chillies, deseeded and finely chopped
4 garlic cloves, finely chopped
2 tomatoes, peeled, deseeded and diced

300g • 10oz fresh shrimps, shelled
30g • 1oz fresh coriander, chopped
juice of 1 lime
salt and freshly ground black pepper

❶ Heat the oil in a pan and gently fry the onion, chillies and garlic for about 5 minutes, stirring occasionally, until softened.
❷ Stir in the tomatoes, shrimps, coriander and lime juice and continue frying gently for a further 3–4 minutes, stirring occasionally until the shrimps turn pink. Season to taste and serve warm or at room temperature.

AFRICAN AUBERGINE DIP

This creamy sauce is a speciality of northern Africa. Serve it at room temperature with hot toast for a tasty starter.

SERVES 6

4 tbsp olive oil
1 large aubergine, diced
1 onion, roughly chopped
2 garlic cloves, roughly chopped
1 red chilli, deseeded and finely chopped
1 tsp ground cumin

¼ tsp turmeric
3 tomatoes, roughly chopped
freshly squeezed juice of 1 lime
2 tbsp chopped fresh parsley
salt and freshly ground black pepper
natural yogurt, to serve

❶ Fry the aubergine in 3 tbsp oil for 5 minutes on each side, until tender and golden. Remove with a slotted spoon and drain well on kitchen paper.
❷ Heat the remaining oil in the same pan, add the onion, garlic and chilli and gently cook, stirring occasionally, for 3 minutes. Add the cumin and turmeric and cook for a further 2 minutes, until the onions are softened.
❸ Stir in the tomatoes, lime juice, parsley and aubergine chunks and cook very gently for 15 minutes, mashing down with a fork until thick and pulpy. Season to taste. Allow to cool, then chill until ready to serve with natural yogurt.

Fresh Shrimp Salsa

OKRA SALSA

Here's a spicy salsa that makes a super accompaniment to smoked meats and seafood. If you wish, add a handful of cooked, peeled prawns.

SERVES 6

4 tbsp palm oil
250g • 8oz okra, sliced into thin rounds
2 onions, finely chopped
1cm • ½in piece root ginger, finely grated
1 red chilli, deseeded and finely chopped

2 garlic cloves, finely chopped
1 tsp ground mixed spice
½ tsp turmeric
2 tomatoes, peeled, deseeded and diced
2 tbsp chopped fresh coriander
salt and freshly ground black pepper

❶ Heat the oil in a large saucepan. Add the okra, onions, ginger, chilli, garlic and spices and stir-fry for 5 minutes. Add the tomatoes and 3 tbsp water, cover and cook very gently for 15 minutes, until the okra is tender.
❷ Stir in the coriander and season to taste. Serve hot.

Tangy Orange Ketchup

This ketchup makes a superb accompaniment
and works well as a marinade or glaze for roasted,
grilled or barbecued fish and chicken. For a sweeter
ketchup, peel the fruit before using.

MAKES 1.2 LITRES/2 PINTS

2 oranges
4 limes
8 garlic cloves
2 red chillies, deseeded and
  finely chopped
430g • 15oz soft brown sugar

475ml • 16fl oz cider vinegar
475ml • 16fl oz apple juice
1 tsp salt
8 whole cloves
8 whole black peppercorns
2 red peppers, deseeded and
  diced

❶ Roughly chop the oranges and limes without peeling
them. Place them in a large saucepan with the garlic,
chillies, sugar, vinegar, apple juice, salt, cloves and peppercorns. Bring to the boil, stirring until the sugar dissolves.
❷ Cover and simmer gently for 45 minutes. Add the peppers
and simmer for a further 45 minutes, until the fruit is soft
and pulpy. Strain the mixture through a fine non-metallic
sieve, then pour immediately into hot, sterilized bottles.
Seal and store.

FRIED PLANTAIN SALSA

Fried plantain chips make a delicious snack in their own right, but remember if you are eating them plain to season them before frying. This tasty salsa cannot wait around to be eaten as the fried plantain soften fairly rapidly.

SERVES 6

2 large under-ripe plantains
vegetable oil for frying
2 tomatoes, diced
1 mango, peeled and diced
4 spring onions, finely chopped
FOR THE DRESSING
1 garlic clove, finely chopped

2 tbsp cider vinegar
2 tbsp vegetable oil
few drops Tabasco sauce or
* 1 tsp chilli sambal*
* (page 61)*
salt and freshly ground black
* pepper*

❶ Slice the plantain very thinly into rings. Put the oil in a heavy-based saucepan and heat until a cube of bread browns in seconds. Deep-fry the plantain slices in the hot oil for 3 minutes until crisp and golden. Drain well on kitchen paper.

❷ Whisk together the dressing ingredients and season to taste.

❸ Toss together the plantain chips, tomatoes, mango, spring onions and dressing and serve immediately.

PIRI-PIRI

Not only is piri-piri very popular for seasoning casseroles in Portugal, it is also a much used condiment in parts of southern Africa. It is used sparingly at the table to bring a little heat and flavour to plainer dishes.

SERVES 8

12 red chillies, deseeded and finely chopped
120ml • 4fl oz vegetable oil
1 tsp fresh oregano, finely chopped

freshly squeezed juice of 1 lemon
salt and freshly ground black pepper

❶ Pound the chillies in a pestle and mortar to make a paste. Gradually whisk in the oil, oregano, lemon juice and salt to taste to make a smooth sauce.
❷ Store, covered, in the fridge for 3–5 days.

CHILLI SAMBAL

Originating in Ghana, chilli sambal is traditionally used to pep up plain rice and vegetable dishes. Spread it sparingly on cuts of fish or meat before char-grilling, or stir a little into simple sauces for extra flavour. It will keep in the fridge, covered, for up to 5 days.

SERVES 8

6 hot red chillies, deseeded and roughly chopped
1 onion, roughly chopped
3 tomatoes, peeled, deseeded and roughly chopped
1 tbsp finely grated fresh root ginger

1 tbsp vegetable oil
grated rind and freshly squeezed juice of 1 lime
salt and freshly ground black pepper

Place all the ingredients in a blender or food processor and whiz together until smooth.

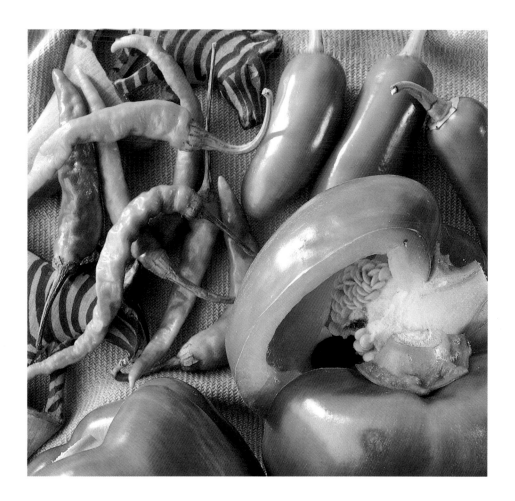

Green Pepper Ketchup

This mildly hot, herby sauce is delicious
splashed on to roasted meat and poultry. It will keep for at
least 6 months if sealed and stored correctly.

MAKES 900ML/1½ PINTS

8 green peppers, deseeded and
    diced

8 green chillies, deseeded and
    halved

1 onion, roughly chopped

2 garlic cloves

2 slices fresh root ginger

1l • 1¾pt malt brown vinegar

430g • 15oz soft brown sugar

1 tbsp black peppercorns

1 tsp salt

❶ Place the peppers, chillies, onion, garlic, ginger, vinegar
and sugar in a large saucepan.

❷ Bring to the boil, stirring until the sugar dissolves. Cover,
lower the heat and simmer very gently, stirring occasionally
for 1½ hours. Strain the mixture through a fine non-metallic
sieve, then pour immediately into hot sterilized bottles. Seal
and store.

HOT GINGER SALSA

This sweet and sour, hot salsa is particularly good
served with fried salt fish. It will only keep in the fridge
for 1 to 2 hours before the flavours and colours fade, so be
sure to eat it soon after it is made.

SERVES 2

7.5cm • 3in piece fresh root
   ginger
1 ripe papaya, peeled and
   roughly diced
2 garlic cloves, finely chopped

2 fresh red chillies, deseeded
   and finely chopped
freshly squeezed juice of 1
   lemon
salt and freshly ground black
   pepper

❶ Peel the ginger and grate it very finely. Place the papaya
flesh in a bowl and mash it smooth with a fork.
❷ Stir in the ginger, garlic, chillies, lemon juice and seasoning to taste. Cover and chill until needed.

LIME SAUCE

This stimulating sauce is delicious added
to groundnut oil and tossed with a crisp green salad or
sprinkled over plainly steamed or grilled seafood.

SERVES 4

2 garlic cloves
4 green chillies, deseeded
3 tbsp fresh coriander leaves
2 tbsp light soy sauce

3 tbsp caster sugar
freshly squeezed juice of
   1 lime

Place the garlic, chillies, coriander and soy sauce in a
blender or food processor and whiz until smooth. Add the
sugar and about 6 tbsp water, stirring until the sugar has
dissolved. Stir in the lime juice and chill until required.

ASIA

THE PREDOMINANT CHARACTERISTIC OF *Asian food is pungent, strong flavours imparted by aromatic spices, including ginger. Alongside the spices, other flavours also feature, particularly chilli, lemon grass, soy sauce, fish sauces and shrimp paste. For the majority of the peasant population, the main source of protein in their diet is salted and dried fish, from which the powerful salty sauces and pastes that are used to flavour ketchups and salsas are derived.*

Natural sugars from coconut paired with vinegar and sharp citrus and sour fruits, such as tamarind, give food the typical Asian sweet and sour taste, and salty sauces combined with hot chillies create another flavour typical of the region.

ASIAN INGREDIENTS

The floating market in Bangkok offers a wealth of fresh fruit and vegetables.

BASIL

A key ingredient in Thai and Vietnamese cookery, basil is a member of the mint family and appears in a number of different varieties, the most popular of which is the green "sweet" basil, readily available in most western countries. Purple, or Opal, basil has a mild flavour that intensifies on cooking; it is more difficult to find outside of Asia but can be easily grown in a window box.

CHILLIES

The general rule with chillies is that the smaller and thinner skinned the chillie is, the hotter it will be. Unlike the mild, thick-skinned Mexican Jalapeño pepper, familiar in the west, Asian chillies are small, pointy and packed with seeds. I advise you to shake out all of the seeds before adding chopped chillies to any dish, for however fiery you like your food, the seeds are very powerful, probably much more so than you are used to. These types of chillies can be bought in Asian grocers, but you must take care when handling them as they can severely irritate the skin. If you have sensitive skin, you should wear rubber gloves.

LEMON GRASS

This thick, almost woody grass is used throughout South East Asia to impart a subtle lemon flavour to soups, stocks and curries. It is available fresh from specialist grocers and large supermarkets, and can be kept, loosely wrapped, in the refrigerator for up to 10 days.

FISH SAUCE

Strong and salty fish sauce is made in much the same way as soy sauce (see below). The liquid that is filtered off after fish and salt have been left to ferment is the thin, dark brown sauce that plays such an important role in the cuisines of Thailand, Vietnam and Burma. In fact, it is served as a condiment with most meals in Vietnam, and with the addition of a little ground chilli, ground nuts or sugar makes a super dipping sauce.

GINGER

One of the most popular spices in Asian cooking, ginger is used fresh or pickled. When fresh, the root is peeled and thinly sliced or grated for inclusion in soups, stir-fries, ketchups and sauces. In China and Japan, however, young roots are thinly sliced and pickled in vinegar. During the process a chemical reaction turns the ginger a delicate shade of pink, and it is often served as garnish to dishes such as sushi. You can find pickled ginger in oriental supermarkets.

Bunches of chillies hung from a wall to dry naturally in the sun.

SHRIMP PASTE

Shrimp paste is made by pulverizing salted shrimps. The paste is then compressed and dried into blocks that are stored in oil to avoid the strong odours that naturally accompany it.

SOY SAUCE

A sweet, salty sauce, soy sauce has been used in China for thousands of years. Made from fermented soy beans and roasted grains (usually wheat, but occasionally barley), it is left to mature in wooden casks for a number of months before being filtered and bottled. It is a vital ingredient in Chinese and Japanese cookery and is also used as a condiment at the table. There are a great number of different soy sauces, including dark and light soy sauces, tamari, shoyu *and* kecap.

JAPANESE GRAPEFRUIT SALSA

This refreshing salsa is a real palate-cleanser, and is wonderful served after a hot or spicy dish.

SERVES 4

2 grapefruit, segmented
1 punnet fresh raspberries
1 tsp black peppercorns

120ml · 4fl oz sake
handful fresh basil leaves, shredded
¼ tsp salt

❶ Cut each segment into 3 even, bite-sized pieces, then place in serving bowl with the raspberries.
❷ Lightly pound the peppercorns in a pestle and mortar, then transfer to a small bowl. Stir in the sake, basil and salt and pour the dressing over the grapefruit salsa. Toss together well. Cover and chill for 1 hour before serving.

RED PEPPER SAMBAL

This spicy sambal is very popular in Indonesia, where it is served on the side with almost every meal. Keep it in a screw-top jar in the fridge for up to a week.

MAKES ABOUT 250G/½LB

1 large red pepper, weighing about 250g · ½lb, deseeded and roughly chopped
1 tsp shrimp paste
1 tsp chilli flakes

4 tbsp sunflower oil
1 tsp dark brown sugar
½ tsp salt
freshly squeezed juice of 1 lime

❶ Whiz the pepper, shrimp paste and chilli flakes together in a food processor until smooth and well blended.
❷ Heat the sunflower oil in a wok or frying pan and stir-fry the pepper mixture for about 5 minutes, until it becomes dark red and the oil separates. Add the sugar and salt and stir until dissolved.
❸ Stir in the lime juice and remove the pan from the heat. Allow the sambal to cool, then cover and chill until ready to use.

Japanese Grapefruit Salsa

SPICY THAI SALSA

This salsa is very potent, so only a small amount is needed.

SERVES 6

6 shallots, halved
6 garlic cloves
6 green chillies
1 tbsp sunflower oil
1 large tomato, deseeded and
    cut into tiny dice

1 tsp shrimp paste
1 tbsp fish sauce
2 tbsp freshly squeezed lime
    juice
salt and freshly ground black
    pepper

❶ Pre-heat the grill to high. Brush the shallots, garlic and green chillies with the oil and then place under the grill for 8 minutes, turning them over once, until tender and a little charred. Roughly chop the shallots and garlic and place in a serving bowl.

❷ Carefully cut open the chillies and shake out and discard the seeds. Finely chop the chilli flesh and set aside.

❸ Stir the tomato dice into the shallot mixture. Whisk together the shrimp paste, fish sauce, lime juice and chopped chilli. Spoon the mixture over the vegetables and toss together well. Check the seasoning and serve warm or at room temperature.

SATAY SAUCE

Satay sauce is traditionally served with skewered
meat and chicken, but I also find a heaped tablespoonful
makes a welcome addition to vegetable stir-fries.

SERVES 4

50g • 2oz creamed coconut
3 tbsp smooth peanut butter
1 tbsp soy sauce
*2 tbsp freshly squeezed lemon
  juice*

*1 tbsp raw peanuts, skinned
  and roughly chopped*
*salt and freshly ground black
  pepper*

❶ Heat the creamed coconut with the peanut butter, soy
sauce and lemon juice in a small saucepan. Gradually whisk
in 150ml/¼ pint boiling water to make a smooth, thick sauce.
❷ Dry-fry the chopped peanuts in a non-stick frying pan for
2–4 minutes, until golden, then stir into the sauce. Season
to taste and serve warm.

JAPANESE SAKE SAUCE

Brush this sweet glazing sauce onto chicken
or fish about halfway through roasting to give a sweet and
salt, crisp, shiny coat.

MAKES ABOUT 300ML/½ PINT

150ml • ¼pt shoyu sauce
6 tbsp caster sugar

*150ml • ¼pt sake (Japanese
  rice wine)*

❶ Place the shoyu sauce, sugar and sake in a small
saucepan and bring to the boil. Lower the heat and simmer
gently, stirring occasionally, for 5 minutes, until the sauce
turns slightly syrupy.
❷ Use immediately, or allow to cool and use as a marinade
for fish or tofu.

HOT AND SOUR SALSA

This piquant salsa is made with white radish –
look out for it in the stores labelled as mooli or daikon.
For an authentic Japanese touch, peel the broccoli
stalk, slice it thickly on the diagonal and add
to the salsa along with the florets.

SERVES 6

*1 head broccoli, head cut into
tiny florets and stalk sliced
(see above)*
2 carrots, cut into sticks
*1 small white radish, peeled
and diced*

FOR THE DRESSING
*3 small red chillies, deseeded
and finely chopped*
1 garlic clove
2 tbsp soy sauce
*freshly squeezed juice of 1
lemon*
1 tsp caster sugar
salt

❶ Place the broccoli florets and slices, if adding, carrot
sticks and radish cubes in a serving bowl.
❷ To make the dressing, pound the chillies and garlic
together in a pestle and mortar to form a paste. Stir in the
soy sauce, lemon juice, sugar and salt to taste.
❸ Add the dressing to the bowl and toss the salsa together
well. Cover and chill for 2 hours before serving.

LONG BEAN SALSA

If you cannot get hold of long beans,
French green beans will do.

SERVES 4

*bunch long beans, weighing
about 125g • ¼lb*
1 tbsp sesame seeds
*6 slices pickled ginger, finely
shredded*

2 tbsp light soy sauce
*2 tbsp freshly squeezed
lemon juice*
salt

❶ Trim the beans and cut into lengths about 2.5cm/1in
long. Plunge into a pan of boiling salted water for exactly 1
minute. Drain and cool completely under cold running
water. Drain well again and place in a bowl.
❷ Place the sesame seeds in a non-stick frying pan and dry-
roast for 1–2 minutes, until golden. Add to the bowl of beans
with the pickled ginger, soy sauce, lemon juice and salt to
taste.
❸ Toss the salsa together well. Cover and chill for 1–2 hours
or until ready to serve.

Hot and Sour Salsa

CUCUMBER *AND* CARROT ACAR

An *acar* is an Asian salsa made from vegetables tossed with vinegar and spices. This fresh-tasting Thai *acar* with its clean taste is a good accompaniment to rich fish and meat dishes. Keep it covered, in the fridge, for up to 2 days.

SERVES 4–6

1 cucumber
1 carrot, cut into tiny dice
3 small Asian chillies, deseeded
   and finely chopped
1 tbsp chopped spring onions
2 tbsp fish sauce
2 tbsp white vinegar
1 tbsp sugar

❶ Peel the cucumber and cut it in half lengthways. Using a teaspoon, scoop out and discard the seeds.
❷ Thinly slice the cucumber into half-moon shapes, then place them in a bowl with the remaining ingredients.
❸ Toss together well. Serve immediately or cover and chill for use later.

CURRIED CAULIFLOWER SALSA

This Indian-style starter makes a delicious accompaniment served with crispy poppadums and red-onion raita. If using frozen peas in place of fresh, add them at step 2 with the lemon juice.

SERVES 4

1 tbsp vegetable oil
1 onion, finely chopped
2 garlic cloves, finely chopped
1 tsp cumin seeds
1 red chilli, deseeded and finely
   chopped
225g • 8oz small cauliflower
   florets
2 ripe tomatoes, roughly
   chopped
50g • 2oz peas
juice of a lemon
1 tsp turmeric
2 tbsp chopped fresh coriander
seasoning

❶ Heat the oil in a wok or large frying pan and add the onion, garlic, cumin, chilli, cauliflower, tomatoes and peas and stir fry for 5 minutes, adding a little more oil or a tablespoon of the lemon juice if the mixture is too dry.
❷ Stir in the turmeric and lemon juice and season to taste. Cook for a further 2 minutes then stir in the coriander. Serve immediately or allow to cool and reheat to serve.

Red-Onion Raita To make red onion raita, stir a small finely chopped red onion and a handful of chopped mint into a pot of natural yogurt. Season with salt, to taste.

Cucumber and Carrot Acar

THAI TOMATO SAUCE

This mouth-watering tomato sauce makes a super accompaniment to fried starters and nibbles, such as pancake rolls or crab cakes. Keep any leftover sauce, covered, in the fridge for two to three days.

SERVES 6

450g • 1lb tomatoes, peeled, deseeded and roughly chopped
1 tbsp sunflower oil
2 tsp sesame oil
1 tbsp tamarind paste (see below)

handful fresh basil leaves
1 stalk fresh lemon grass
2 tbsp dark soy sauce
1 tsp hot chilli sauce
salt and freshly ground black pepper

❶ Place all the ingredients in a saucepan, cover and simmer gently, stirring occasionally, for 45 minutes, until thick and pulpy.
❷ Strain the sauce through a fine non-metallic sieve and return to the rinsed-out pan. Season to taste and heat through. Serve hot.

TAMARIND PASTE

To make tamarind paste, beat a heaped tbsp of standard tamarind pulp with 3 tbsp boiling water. Pass the mixture through a fine non-metallic sieve to give a smooth, very thick sauce. Store in the fridge for up to a week. You can buy tamarind paste at oriental supermarkets.

ALL-PURPOSE DIPPING SAUCE

This incredibly versatile dipping sauce can be
served with any number of dishes. Try it with fried or
steamed cubes of tofu or strips of grilled meat.

SERVES 4

*4 tbsp shoyu or other high-
quality soy sauce*
2 tbsp white wine vinegar

1 tbsp sesame oil
1 tsp dark brown sugar
1 tsp chilli flakes

Blend all the ingredients together with 1 tbsp water.

VARIATIONS Add any one or a combination of the following for
a good variation of the All-Purpose Dipping Sauce:

*chopped fresh coriander or
basil*
toasted sesame seeds
finely diced tomato

crushed garlic clove
grated cucumber
finely chopped fresh green chilli
finely chopped spring onion

CARIBBEAN

THE STORMY, TROPICAL CLIMATE *of the Caribbean islands produces a wealth of exotic fruit and vegetables, which, combined with aromatic herbs and spices, produce a highly distinctive cuisine. Gathering influences from many different sources, including West Africa and Europe, Caribbean food is fresh and exciting. It uses a mélange of traditional and historical methods of cooking and is continually taking in new combinations of flavours.*

A fundamental aspect of family eating is the buffet with many dishes served together on one table ~ you will find plainer rice, bean and cornmeal dishes enlivened by bowls of vibrant salsas and colourful ketchups. And many typical dishes, such as Jamaican jerk chicken, involve marinating and brushing meat, fish and poultry with fresh herbs and spices, establishing a need for flavoursome ketchups and sauces.

CARIBBEAN INGREDIENTS

BANANA

Sweet, ripe bananas are an essential ingredient in tropical food. They are at their best when deep yellow with just a few, if any, black spots. Don't choose bananas that are blackened and soft. If using them raw, squeeze a little fresh lemon or lime juice over the cut surfaces to help prevent browning.

COCONUT

Fresh coconuts are readily available from grocery stores on the Islands. When choosing yours, shake it to make sure it has plenty of juice inside – a good sign of freshness. Crack the shell and shake out all the liquid, then peel off the papery skin and dice, grate, shave or chop the flesh. To make coconut

Plump purple aubergines and orange-fleshed squashes are examples of the region's colourful and distinctive ingredients.

Exotic fruit for sale in a Jamaican market.

milk, chop the flesh and place it in a bowl, then cover with boiling water and leave to cool completely. Strain the liquid through a muslin cloth, and it is then ready to use in a whole host of dishes, such as soups, curries and drinks to name just a few. You can also buy creamed coconut in blocks which can be crumbled into a dish; coconut cream and coconut milk and dried dessicated coconut can be used to make coconut milk in the same way as fresh. Rich in protein, vitamins and oil, coconut has a high nutritional value, however, unlike nut and vegetable oils, coconut oil is a saturated fat with a high cholesterol content, so it should be eaten sparingly.

Lemon

The sharp tang of lemons makes them unsuitable to eat as a fruit, but they are used to flavour inummerable sweet and savoury dishes, as well as in baking and making marmalades, chutneys and ketchups. Lemon juice also helps to prevent the natural discoloration (enzymic browning) of certain fruits, such as pear and avocado, when the cut surface is exposed to the air – this is particularly useful to remember if you are planning to prepare fruit a little while in advance of serving.

Mango

Originally from Asia, the mango is now closely associated with Caribbean food. It is not really possible to judge the ripeness of a mango by the colour of its skin, as some are ripe even when green. To test for ripeness, squeeze the flesh gently and it should give slightly; do not choose mangoes that are hard or have wrinkled or black, blotchy skins. Take care that your knife doesn't slip when you slice the flesh from the large, flat, slippery stone before peeling and dicing the sweet flesh. Use raw in desserts or cooked in hot salsas and ketchups.

MELON SALSA

This sweet and sour salsa uses a
blend of white rum, golden sugar and fresh lemon juice to
give a tropical taste of the Caribbean.

SERVES 4

*1 small sweet melon, such as
    Charentais or Galia, peeled,
    deseeded and diced*
4 tbsp white rum
1 small red onion, finely diced
*1 green chilli, deseeded and
    finely chopped*

2 tbsp fresh coriander
1 tsp golden sugar
*freshly squeezed juice of ½
    lemon*
*salt and freshly ground black
    pepper*

❶ Place the melon and rum in a large bowl, cover and chill
for 1–2 hours, stirring gently once or twice.
❷ When ready to serve, stir in the onion, chilli, coriander,
sugar, lemon juice and seasoning to taste.

TROPICAL SALSA

Serve this sunny salsa as part of a meal or,
if planning a dinner party, this quantity will serve 4
as a light starter.

SERVES 4

1 large ripe papaya, diced
1 large ripe avocado, diced
*2 thick slices fresh pineapple,
    cored and diced*
2 tbsp soy sauce
*grated rind and freshly
    squeezed juice of 1 orange*
2 tbsp groundnut oil

2 tbsp dark brown sugar
1 garlic clove, finely chopped
*1cm • ½in fresh root ginger,
    finely grated*
½ tsp chilli flakes
4 tbsp chopped fresh coriander
4 tbsp chopped fresh mint
*salt and freshly ground black
    pepper*

❶ Place the papaya, avocado and pineapple in a large bowl.
❷ Mix together the soy sauce, orange juice, oil and sugar,
stirring until the sugar has dissolved. Whisk in the garlic,
ginger, chilli flakes, orange rind, coriander and mint and
season to taste.
❸ Pour the dressing over the fruit and toss together well.
Cover and chill for 1–2 hours before serving.

Melon Salsa

JAMAICAN JERK SAUCE

Throughout the Caribbean, jerk sauce is rubbed on to meat before it is barbecued or grilled. Jerk seasonings and sauces always contain a special combination of spices which includes cinnamon, nutmeg and allspice. If you prefer a slightly more pungent sauce, don't grill the spring onions but use them raw.

SERVES 6

6 spring onions
4 tbsp fresh thyme, roughly
    chopped
4 garlic cloves, roughly chopped
1cm • ¼in piece fresh root
    ginger, roughly chopped
3 red chillies, deseeded and
    finely chopped

½ tsp grated nutmeg
¼ tsp ground cinnamon
1 tsp ground allspice
4 tbsp soy sauce
2 tbsp malt vinegar
salt and freshly ground black
    pepper

❶ Preheat the grill. Grill the spring onions for 5 minutes, turning them once, until tender and a little charred. Chop finely.

❷ Pound together the thyme, garlic, ginger and chillies in a pestle and mortar to form a paste. Pound in the chopped spring onions.

❸ Stir in the ground spices, soy sauce, malt vinegar and seasoning to taste.

Lemon *and* Lime Ketchup

This ketchup takes six months to mature before it's ready to serve, but the tangy citrus flavour is excellent for salad dressings, marinades and soups, so it's worth the wait.

MAKES 1.2 LITRES/2 PINTS

4 lemons
4 limes
6 tbsp salt
1 onion, finely chopped
2 garlic cloves, finely chopped
900ml • 1½pt white wine
   vinegar

1 tsp whole cloves, lightly
   crushed
1 tbsp ground ginger
1 tsp whole black peppercorns,
   lightly crushed

❶ Peel the lemons and limes and slice them thickly. Rub the salt into the flesh and layer in hot sterilized jars with the onion and garlic.
❷ Place the vinegar, cloves, ginger and peppercorns in a saucepan and bring to the boil. Pour over the lemons, seal with vinegar-proof lids and store for 6 months.
❸ Strain the ketchup into sterilized bottles. Seal and store for up to 12 months.

PASSIONATE SALSA

Serve this fruity salsa with hot
pancakes or creamy yogurt for a flavoursome dessert or
weekend breakfast. Serve chilled.

SERVES 4

4 pomegranates
4 passion fruit
*2.5cm • 1in piece stem
    ginger in syrup*
*2 tbsp syrup from the jar
    of ginger*

freshly squeezed juice of 1 lime
1 tbsp groundnut oil
*1 tsp whole black peppercorns,
    lightly crushed*
1 tsp brown sugar
1 tbsp chopped fresh mint
¼ tsp coarse salt

❶ Cut the pomegranates and passion fruit in half and scoop
out the flesh and seeds into a bowl.
❷ Finely chop the stem ginger and mix with the ginger
syrup, lime juice and groundnut oil. Spoon over the fruit and
mix together well. Cover and chill until ready to serve.
❸ When ready to serve, divide the salsa into individual
serving dishes and sprinkle with the pepper, sugar, mint
and salt.

PEACH *AND* RAISIN SALSA

Add a touch of spice to this peachy salsa by stirring
in ½ tsp of ground cinnamon at step 3.

SERVES 4

8 peaches, halved and stoned
2 tbsp vegetable oil
1 large onion, finely chopped
2.5cm • 1in piece fresh root
 ginger, finely grated
215g • 7½oz soft brown sugar
75g • 2½oz raisins

120ml • 4fl oz freshly squeezed
 orange juice
120ml • 4fl oz red wine
 vinegar
salt and freshly ground black
 pepper

❶ Preheat the grill to medium. Lightly brush the peaches
with oil and place under the grill for 15 minutes, turning
once, until tender and golden.

❷ Meanwhile, heat the remaining oil in a small saucepan,
add the onion and ginger and cook gently, stirring occasionally, for 5 minutes, until softened.

❸ Cut the peaches into small pieces and add to the pan
with the sugar, raisins, orange juice and vinegar. Bring to the
boil, then cover, lower the heat and simmer for 40 minutes.

❹ Season to taste and allow to cool completely. Store in the
fridge, covered, for up to 10 days.

PINEAPPLE SALSA

This fruity Caribbean salsa tastes super with grilled chicken and fried salt-cod fish cakes. It can be kept, covered, in the fridge for up to 2 days.

SERVES 4–6

175g • 6oz fresh peeled and cored pineapple, cut into small dice
2 tbsp chopped fresh coriander grated rind and freshly squeezed juice of ½ lime

1cm • ½in piece fresh root ginger, finely grated
1 tsp light brown sugar
salt and freshly ground black pepper

❶ Place the pineapple, coriander, lime juice and rind and ginger in a large bowl and toss together well.
❷ Stir in the sugar and season to taste with salt and pepper.
❸ Cover and chill in the fridge for at least 2 hours until ready to serve.

PAN-FRIED FRUIT SALSA

Turn this savoury salsa into a sweet one by omitting the garlic and chilli and adding a tablespoon or two of honey in place of the Tabasco.

SERVES 4

1 tsp vegetable oil
1 garlic clove, thinly sliced
1 red chilli, deseeded and thinly sliced
2 thick slices fresh pineapple, cut into chunks

2 green mangoes, cubed
4 tbsp fresh pineapple juice
few drops Tabasco seasoning

❶ Heat the oil in a wok or large frying pan and stir fry the garlic, chilli, pineapple and mango over a high heat for 5 minutes until golden brown.
❷ Add the pineapple juice and Tabasco and heat through for 2 minutes until piping hot. Season to taste and serve immediately.

Sweet Potato
and Coconut Salsa

For a simple and tasty tropical supper, brush 4 small fish such as red snapper with a little oil and roast in the oven with the salsa for the final 20 minutes. Serve the fish with the salsa and some crisp green salad on the side.

SERVES 4

500g • 1lb sweet potatoes, cubed
2 tbsp vegetable oil
400g • 14oz can pineapple chunks in natural juice, drained
475g • 16fl oz thick coconut milk

freshly squeezed juice of ½ lemon
1 red chilli, deseeded and finely chopped
salt and freshly ground black pepper

❶ Preheat the oven to 200°C/400°F/Gas 6. Place the sweet potato in a roasting tin and drizzle over the oil and a little seasoning. Roast in the oven for 20 minutes.

❷ Stir in the pineapple chunks, coconut milk, lemon juice, chilli and seasoning. Return to the oven and roast for a further 20 minutes, until the potatoes are tender and the salsa has thickened.

BANANA AND GINGER KETCHUP

This tropical ketchup is perfect
to serve with grilled chicken and fish or with a
platter of tangy cheese.

MAKES 900ML/1½ PINTS

*10 ripe bananas, peeled and
  roughly chopped*
2 onions, finely chopped
*5cm • 2in piece root ginger,
  finely grated*

600ml • 1pt cider vinegar
400g • 14oz soft brown sugar
2 tsp black peppercorns
1 tsp allspice berries
1tsp salt

❶ Place the bananas, onions, ginger, vinegar, sugar, spices
and salt in a large saucepan. Bring to the boil, stirring until
the sugar dissolves. Cover and simmer gently for 1 hour, stirring occasionally, until thick and pulpy.
❷ Strain the mixture through a fine non-metallic sieve,
then pour immediately into hot sterilized bottles. Seal and
store for up to 6 months.

HOT MANGO SALSA

Serve this fiery salsa with a bowl
of tortilla chips for an irresistible party dip.

SERVES 4

1 tbsp vegetable oil
1 large onion, finely chopped
2 green chillies, deseeded and
  finely chopped
2 ripe mangoes, peeled and
  diced

2 ripe tomatoes, diced
freshly squeezed juice of 2 limes
1 tbsp soft brown sugar
salt and freshly ground black
  pepper

❶ Heat the oil in a small saucepan and gently cook the
onion and chillies for 5 minutes until softened.
❷ Add the mangoes and tomatoes, cover and cook very
gently for 30 minutes.
❸ Stir in the lime juice and sugar and season to taste,
adding more sugar if necessary. Serve hot or cold.

SOUTH AMERICA

AS WELL AS COVERING *South America*, this chapter also includes Mexico – the home of the salsa. For that reason, there are only salsa recipes here, many of which are classical dishes that you may have tried before. Serve these salsas with sizzling chicken or prawn fajitas and as tastebud-tickling dipping sauces for fiery tortilla chips, crispy tacos and cheese nachos.

The two most valuable ingredients of this culinary region are corn, which is used to make, among many other things, the essential tortilla, and chillies, which are the most crucial component of almost all salsas.

SOUTH AMERICAN *and* MEXICAN INGREDIENTS

Giant scallions and fresh limes on a Mexican market.

JALAPEÑO

The jalapeño *is a very popular ingredient in both raw and cooked salsas. It is relatively large and plump with dark green, thick flesh that is medium hot. When dried, the jalapeño turns a rusty brown colour and is then known as a* chipotle *chilli.*

PEQUIN

This tiny, dark red chilli is extremely fiery. Usually only available dried whole or in flakes, it should be used sparingly in sauces or added to flasks of oil to make chilli oil. Never attempt to eat a whole pequin.

POBLANO

This large chilli and the pasilla *are very similar. It is mild – medium hot with a rich, distinctive flavour. It is very popular dried, when it becomes very wrinkled and acquires a smoky taste. Dried* poblanoes *may be dark red, when they are known as* ancho, *or dark brown and known as* mulato.

In Mexico, the home of salsa, there's no shortage of fresh and flavoursome produce.

SUNSHINE SALSA

This beautiful salsa really does
bring a ray of sunshine to the dining table. Serve as a
refreshing accompaniment to fish.

SERVES 4

2 yellow tomatoes, thinly sliced
2 ripe red tomatoes, thinly
* sliced*
2 small oranges, peeled and
* thinly sliced into rounds*
1 tsp bottled pink peppercorns,
* lightly crushed*

1 garlic clove, finely chopped
2 tbsp chopped fresh parsley,
* coriander or chives*
2 tbsp extra-virgin olive oil
salt and freshly ground black
* pepper*

❶ Arrange the tomatoes and orange slices on a large round
serving platter.
❷ Whisk together the peppercorns, garlic, herbs, olive oil
and plenty of seasoning. Drizzle over the salsa and serve
immediately.

CHIMICHURRI

This is a South American classic. Popular in Argentina and
Brazil, chimichurri is a simple salsa based on onions,
parsley and chilli. It is traditionally served with
plain grilled or barbecued meats.

SERVES 6

*2 red onions or 4 purple
  shallots, finely chopped*
*2 hot red chillies, deseeded and
  finely chopped*
*1 large garlic clove, finely
  chopped*
4 tbsp chopped fresh parsley
2 tbsp olive oil
*freshly squeezed juice of 1
  lemon*
*salt and freshly ground black
  pepper*

Place all the ingredients in a large bowl and toss together
well. Season to taste, cover and chill for 1–2 hours before
serving.

SALSA VERDE

Like *salsa cruda* there are many
different types of green salsa. The ingredients are
traditionally chopped by hand, but if you prefer a smoother
salsa, whiz them in a minifood processor or blender.

SERVES 6

6 spring onions, finely chopped
1 onion, finely chopped
2 garlic cloves, finely chopped
2 green chillies, deseeded and
* finely chopped*
6 tbsp chopped fresh coriander
6 tbsp chopped fresh flat-leaf
* parsley*

1 tbsp capers, well drained and
* finely chopped (optional)*
4 tbsp olive oil
freshly squeezed juice and
* grated rind of 1 lemon*
salt and freshly ground black
* pepper*

Place all the ingredients in a large serving bowl and toss
together well. Season to taste and serve immediately.

HOT GUACAMOLE

Like all South American salsas, this one
makes a brilliant dipping sauce for nachos
and tortilla chips.

SERVES 4

2 garlic cloves, roughly chopped
2 red chillies, deseeded and
* roughly chopped*
6 black peppercorns

2 large avocados
2 tbsp olive oil
juice of a lemon
salt

❶ Pound the garlic, chillies and peppercorns in a pestle and
mortar to make paste.
❷ Peel and stone the avocados and mash the flesh well. Stir
in the chilli paste, olive oil and lemon juice. Season to taste,
cover and refrigerate until ready to serve.

PICO DE GALLO

There are many versions of this
Mexican salsa, whose title translates as rooster's beak.
Here's my version, which is best spooned on to cheese-
covered tacos and burritos or drizzled over
sizzling chicken or beef.

SERVES 6

4 tomatoes, roughly chopped
1 red onion, finely chopped
10 radishes, roughly chopped
2 green chillies, deseeded and
  finely chopped

2 tbsp chopped fresh coriander
freshly squeezed juice of 1 lime
¼ tsp salt

Place all the ingredients together in a large bowl and toss
together well. Serve immediately.

SALSA CON QUESO

This dish is always on the menu in Mexican-style restaurants and simply needs tortillas or tacos to make a complete snack-meal for two.

SERVES 2

1 tbsp vegetable oil
1 small onion, finely chopped
2 garlic cloves, finely chopped
4 rashers streaky bacon, rinded and roughly chopped
400g • 14oz can chopped plum tomatoes

2 tsp chilli flakes
½ tsp salt
100g • 4oz full-flavoured cheese, such as mature Cheddar or Monterey jack, grated

❶ Heat the oil in a pan and gently cook the onion, garlic and bacon for about 5 minutes, stirring occasionally, until tender and golden. Add the can of tomatoes, chilli flakes and salt and bring to the boil, then cover and simmer gently for 15 minutes.
❷ Meanwhile, preheat the grill.
❸ Transfer the mixture to a shallow flameproof dish and scatter over the cheese. Place under the grill for about 5 minutes, until bubbling and golden. Serve immediately.

SALSA CRUDA

There are endless raw South American
salsas, all going under the name of *salsa cruda*; this is
a very simple version that is delicious scooped
up with tortilla chips for a snack
or served as part of a meal.

SERVES 4

*2 large tomatoes, roughly
chopped*

*8 spring onions, roughly
chopped*

*2 hot green chillies, deseeded
and finely chopped*

*2 tbsp chopped fresh parsley or
coriander*

*freshly squeezed juice of ½
lemon*

1 tbsp olive oil

*salt and freshly ground black
pepper*

Place all the ingredients in a large bowl and toss together
well. Season to taste, cover and chill for at least 2 hours
before serving.

ROASTED HABANERO SALSA

Habanero, or Scotch Bonnets, are one of
the hottest chilli peppers. Unlike other fiery chillies,
they're not just hot but they are flavoursome, too.
Mix a little of this salsa with plain pasta or rice.

SERVES 4

6 ripe plum tomatoes, halved
5 tbsp extra-virgin olive oil
4 garlic cloves, crushed
10 habanero chilli peppers
1 red onion, finely chopped

freshly squeezed juice of 1
  lemon
2 tbsp chopped fresh coriander
salt and freshly ground black
  pepper

❶ Preheat the oven to 240°C/475°F/Gas 9. Arrange the
tomatoes, cut side up, on a baking sheet and drizzle with 1
tbsp olive oil. Sprinkle with a little garlic, salt and black
pepper, then roast for 15 minutes, until beginning to char.

❷ Meanwhile, skewer the chillies with a fork and hold
them one at a time on the flame of a gas ring for about 3
minutes, until blistered. When they are all blistered, slip off
the skins and chop the flesh finely. If you don't have gas,
place the chillies under a hot grill for 5–6 minutes, turning
once.

❸ Dice the tomatoes and place them in a bowl with the
chopped chillies, remaining olive oil and garlic, red onion,
lemon juice, coriander and a little seasoning. Keep covered
in the refrigerator for up to 5 days, or until required.

SALSA CALIENTE

This sauce is the base of many dishes such as Oaxacan Eggs, a speciality of the Mexican state of Oaxaca, where eggs are poached in *salsa caliente* and sprinkled with grated cheese before serving. If you find the sauce too thick, stir in a little hot chicken or vegetable stock. This also makes a very good accompaniment to most meat and fish, and it can be served as a dip.

SERVES 4

*4 large ripe tomatoes, halved
   and deseeded
2 tbsp vegetable oil
2 jalapeño chillies, deseeded
   and finely chopped
2 garlic cloves, finely chopped*

*1 small onion, finely chopped
chicken or vegetable stock,
   optional
salt and freshly ground black
   pepper*

❶ Preheat the grill. Brush the tomato halves with a little oil and grill for about 8 minutes, turning them once, until softened and a little charred. Peel and discard the skin and chop the flesh roughly.

❷ Meanwhile, pound the chillies, garlic and onion using a pestle and mortar until they form a fairly smooth paste.

❸ Heat the remaining oil in a small frying pan and cook the paste and tomatoes gently for about 5 minutes, until thick and pulpy, adding stock if necessary. Season to taste and serve hot or cover and chill for up to 5 days. This salsa freezes well.

TOMATILLO SALSA

If you can find fresh tomatillos, remove the papery skins, halve the tomatillos and simmer them gently in water until tender. This fruity salsa will keep, covered in the refrigerator, for up to 5 days.

SERVES 6

2 fresh papayas, peeled and diced
1 small onion, finely chopped
1 red pepper, deseeded and diced
1 green pepper, deseeded and diced
250g • 8oz can tomatillos, drained and finely chopped

1 small hot red chilli, deseeded and finely chopped
2 tbsp chopped fresh coriander
2 garlic cloves, finely chopped
freshly squeezed juice of 1 orange
2 tbsp olive oil
salt and freshly ground black pepper

❶ Place the papaya, onion and peppers in a bowl.
❷ Mix together the tomatillos, chilli, coriander, garlic, orange juice and olive oil and season well to taste. Add to the papaya mixture and toss together well. Cover and chill until ready to serve.

SWEET ONION SALSA

The sautéeing process in this recipe turns the starches in the onions into sugar, hence a sweet caramelized flavour. This salsa is delicious with tangy cheese and soft bread.

SERVES 4

2 tbsp vegetable oil
4 onions, thinly sliced
2 garlic cloves, finely chopped
2 tbsp chopped fresh parsley

1 tbsp freshly squeezed lemon juice
salt and freshly ground black pepper

❶ Heat the oil in a large frying pan and gently sauté the onions for 20 minutes, until soft and golden brown. Stir in the garlic and cook for a further 2–3 minutes.
❷ Transfer the mixture to a bowl and stir in the parsley and lemon juice and season to taste. Serve warm.

NORTH AMERICA

FROM THE SOPHISTICATED, MEDITERRANEAN-inspired cuisine of California to the traditional Deep South flavours of Louisiana, American food is plentiful and bursting with vitality. And, throughout the States, regional food is truly coming into its own – not only the flavour-packed, and almost vegetarian style of cooking and eating from California, but on the other side of the continent, Florida is undergoing a food revolution, too. There the Latin-American community is playing a major role in the state-wide trend towards the fusion of South American and Jamaican-influenced food.

NORTH AMERICAN INGREDIENTS

Ripe tomatoes are the heart of classic ketchups and salsas.

CORN

Originally from Mexico, corn is an important ingredient in the USA. If eating it on the cob, the best way to cook corn is to simply boil it for about 5 minutes, until the kernels are bright yellow and tender – do not salt the water as it toughens the kernels. Instead season after cooking and brush with melted butter. Another delicious way to cook corn-on-the-cob is to sprinkle on a little fresh lime juice and barbecue it over hot coals. If you want to remove the kernels, use a large, sharp knife to slice them off the cob. Kernels can also be bought cooked and canned or frozen.

CRANBERRIES

Very tart when raw, cranberries are at their best when they are cooked, and they are great made into a ketchup, jam or sauce. Used in place of raisins and dried berries, they are also delicious baked in muffins and fruit pies. They are mainly grown in the USA and are harvested in winter, so look for them in the shops from late October through to early February. Cranberries are extremely robust and store well when fresh but are also available frozen, and more recently in dried form, both of which make very good substitutes for the fresh.

RED ONIONS

Just one member of the enormous onion family, red onions with their sweet and mild flavour are particularly suitable for stirring raw into salsas. Their beautiful red/purple colouring also stands up to heat, making them a valuable addition to cooked ketchups and salsas, too.

TOMATILLOS

Also known as husk tomatoes, green tomatillos come wrapped in a papery skin that needs to be re~~moved~~ before using. Their raw, sour flavour is a valuable ingredient in salsas throughout the States and South America. In fact, tomatillos are often used as the basis of classic salsa *verde. They are available both fresh and canned all over America and can be found in specialist shops in the UK.*

Whether boiled or barbecued, corn is a complement of many North American salsas.

ROASTED PEPPER SALSA

This Californian salsa is very much influenced by the Mediterranean. It is important that the peppers are left covered for 5 minutes after grilling as the gentle steam that results helps lift the skin away from the flesh.

SERVES 4

2 red peppers
2 yellow peppers
2 orange peppers
2 garlic cloves, finely chopped
2 ripe tomatoes, finely diced

2 tbsp chopped fresh flat-leaf parsley
4 tbsp extra-virgin olive oil
3 tbsp balsamic vinegar
salt and freshly ground black pepper

❶ Preheat the grill to medium. Place all the peppers under the grill for about 10 minutes, turning them frequently, until blackened and charred. Cover with a tea towel and leave to cool for 5 minutes.

❷ With the point of a sharp knife, pierce a hole in the bottom of each pepper and squeeze all the juice into a jug. Peel away the skin and discard, then cut the flesh into very thin ½-cm/¼-in thick slices.

❸ Place the warm pepper strips in a serving bowl with the garlic, tomatoes and parsley. Whisk together the pepper juices, olive oil and balsamic vinegar and season to taste. Pour over the peppers and toss together well. Serve while still warm or cover and chill for up to 4 days.

CLASSIC AMERICAN TOMATO KETCHUP

Serve this all-American favourite with just about anything. Try topping cheese on toast with a spoonful of this rich, thick ketchup or simply use it for dipping your fries into.

MAKES ABOUT 1.2L/2PT

1.5kg • 3lb ripe tomatoes, quartered
2 garlic cloves, halved
120ml • 4fl oz cider vinegar
50g • 2oz sugar
½ tsp ground ginger
½ tsp salt
4 black peppercorns
4 cloves

❶ Place the tomatoes and garlic in a large saucepan. Cover and stew down very gently for 1 hour, stirring occasionally, until thick and pulpy.

❷ Purée the tomato pulp in a food processor or blender until smooth, then return it to the washed pan. Add the remaining vinegar, sugar and spices. Bring to the boil, stirring, until the sugar dissolves. Cover and simmer for 45 minutes, stirring until thick and smooth.

❸ Strain the mixture through a fine non-metallic sieve, then pour immediately into hot sterilized bottles. Seal and store until required.

Sweet Cherry Ketchup

Serve this seasonal ketchup with beef burgers or as a dip for crispy fries or onion rings.

MAKES ABOUT 900ML/1½PT

1 onion, roughly chopped
2 large cooking apples, cored, peeled and roughly chopped
900g • 2lb morello cherries, stoned
475ml • 16fl oz red wine vinegar
430g • 15oz soft brown sugar
1-cm • ½-in piece root ginger
½ tsp ground cinnamon
½ tsp salt

❶ Place all the ingredients in a large pan and bring to the boil, stirring until the sugar dissolves. Cover and simmer for 1 hour, stirring occasionally.
❷ Strain the mixture through a fine non-metallic sieve, then pour immediately into hot sterilized bottles. Seal and store until required.

ROASTED CORN SALSA

Fill a baked potato with a spoonful
of soured cream and top with this fragrant salsa for a
super light lunch. Remember to choose the freshest,
juiciest corn cobs.

SERVES 8

4 corn on the cobs
freshly squeezed juice of 2 limes
4 tomatoes, deseeded and finely
    diced
2 red onions, finely chopped

4 tbsp chopped fresh coriander
3 tbsp olive oil
salt and freshly ground black
    pepper

❶ Brush the corn cobs with a little of the lime juice and
sprinkle with salt. Gently barbecue or grill for 20–30 minutes, turning them over occasionally, until tender and
golden. Using a large, heavy knife, slice down the cobs to
remove the kernels.

❷ Place the corn kernels in a bowl with the tomatoes, red
onions and coriander. Whisk together the olive oil and remaining lime juice. Season to taste and pour over the salsa.
Toss well to mix and serve while still slightly warm, or cover
and chill for up to 2 hours.

Instant Tomato Salsa

This speedy salsa takes literally seconds to prepare and
serve as a great dip for corn chips.

SERVES 6

400g • 14oz can tomatoes
1 garlic clove
3 spring onions

few drops Tabasco sauce
salt and freshly ground black
pepper

Place all the ingredients in a food processor or blender and
pulse for a few seconds until smooth. Season to taste, then
pour into an air-tight container and refrigerate for up to 5
days until required.

Barbecue Salsa

Serve this tasty sauce as an accompaniment
to cooked meats or use as a marinade for spareribs.

MAKES ABOUT 900ml/½pt

300ml • ½pt tomato ketchup
1 onion, finely chopped
2 tomatoes, skinned, deseeded
  and finely chopped
2 garlic cloves, finely chopped
1-cm • ½-in piece root ginger,
  finely chopped

150ml • ¼pt freshly squeezed
  orange juice
2 tbsp vegetable oil
3 tbsp soy sauce
3 tbsp honey
1 tsp English mustard

Place all the ingredients in a large saucepan with 450ml/¾pt
water and bring to the boil. Cover and simmer gently for 20
minutes, stirring occasionally. Cool, cover and keep in the
refrigerator for up to 2 weeks. This also freezes well.

Texan Green Tomato Salsa

This fairly fiery salsa should be served chilled. Make it milder or hotter by altering the amounts and type of chilli you use.

SERVES 8

4 green chillies, deseeded and
    finely chopped
4 green tomatoes, roughly
    chopped
2 onions, roughly chopped

2 garlic cloves, finely chopped
1 tbsp chopped fresh oregano,
    or ½ tbsp dried
salt and freshly ground black
    pepper

❶ Place the chillies, tomatoes, onions, garlic and about 300ml/½pt water in a saucepan and bring to the boil. Cover and simmer for 30 minutes, stirring occasionally, until thick and pulpy.

❷ Strain the mixture through a fine non-metallic sieve, then stir in the garlic, oregano and salt and pepper to taste. Cover and chill up to 5 days until required.

WATERMELON SALSA

Bring out the flavour of plain
grilled or roasted seafood, such as lobster or scallops,
with this salsa.

SERVES 6

1 small cucumber
*250g • 8oz watermelon flesh,
 diced*
1 small red onion, thinly sliced
1 tbsp chopped fresh mint
1 tbsp chopped fresh chives

*1 small red chilli, deseeded and
 finely chopped*
*1 small garlic clove, finely
 chopped*
freshly squeezed juice of 1 lime
*salt and freshly ground black
 pepper*

❶ Slice the cucumber in half lengthways, then slice each half widthways to make semi-circles. Place them in a bowl with the watermelon, red onion, mint, chives, chilli, garlic and lime juice.

❷ Season to taste and serve immediately, or cover and chill for up to one day.

BARBECUED SALSA *WITH* HERBED OIL DRESSING

This makes a delicious outdoor meal served with baked potatoes and a spoonful of sour cream.

SERVES 6

4 corn cobs
8 tomatoes, quartered
2 red onions, quartered

HERBED OIL DRESSING

4 tbsp olive oil
2 tbsp balsamic vinegar
*2 tbsp chopped fresh tarragon
seasoning*

❶ Begin by making the herbed oil—stir together the oil, vinegar, herbs, salt and pepper.

❷ Brush the corn cobs with the dressing and place on the barbecue for 20 to 30 minutes. Remove the kernels.

❸ Thread the tomatoes and onions onto skewers and brush with the oil. Barbecue for 15 to 20 minutes until tender.

❹ Transfer the kernels, onions, and tomatoes to a large bowl. Pour over the remaining dressing.

Watermelon Salsa

CRANBERRY KETCHUP

This sweet-and-sour ketchup makes a tasty accompaniment to fried chicken.

MAKES ABOUT 900ML/1½PT

900g • 2lb fresh cranberries
375g • ¾lb sultanas
475ml • 16fl oz red wine
  vinegar
430g • 15oz soft brown sugar
2 tsp ground allspice
1 tsp salt
1 tsp ground cinnamon

❶ Place all the ingredients in a large saucepan and bring to the boil, stirring until the sugar dissolves. Cover and simmer for 1 hour, stirring occasionally.
❷ Strain the mixture through a fine non-metallic sieve, then pour immediately into hot, sterilized bottles. Seal and store until required.

PESTO SALSA

Using the same basic ingredients as
the Italian pasta sauce, this Californian salsa is best served
with fish or poultry. Use to fill the cavities of 4 small fish or
make deep incisions in 4 chicken breasts and spread the
salsa thickly on top before barbecuing or grilling.

SERVES 4

4 tbsp pine nuts
*2 large garlic cloves, finely
    chopped*
*1 small red chilli, deseeded and
    finely chopped*
*2 handfuls fresh basil, finely
    chopped*

*2 tbsp freshly grated Parmesan
    or Pecorino cheese*
4 tbsp extra-virgin olive oil
*freshly squeezed juice and
    grated rind of 1 lemon*
*salt and freshly ground black
    pepper*

❶ Place the pine nuts in a non-stick frying pan and dry fry
for 3–5 minutes until golden. Use a heavy knife to chop
them finely.
❷ Place the nuts in a bowl with the garlic, chilli, basil,
cheese, olive oil and lemon juice and rind and season well
with salt and plenty of black pepper. Use immediately or
cover and chill for up to 2 hours.

INDEX

ACKNOWLEDGEMENTS

Pictor 6, 8–9, Stuart Frawley/Ace 11, Pictor 17, PictureBank 18–19, 21, Mauritius/Ace 23, PictureBank 40–1, Fotopic/Ace 42, Trevor Wood/Image Bank 57, PictureBank 68–9, 70, Zephyr Pictures/Ace 86–7, Allan Stone/Ace 88, Mauritius/Ace 89, Grant V. Faint/Image Bank 98–9, Pictor 100, 108–9, 111, Alan Spence/Ace 118–9, Pictor 120, 122.

All other photographs are the copyright of Quarto Publishing plc. Quarto would also like to thank Lee Pattison and Villeroy & Boch Tableware Ltd, 267 Merton Road, London SW18 5JS; Oddbins UK Ltd, 31 Weir Road Industrial Estate, London SW19 8UG and Agadir Restaurant, 84 Westbourne Grove, London W2 for supplying props for photography.